THE *MAYFLOWER*

A PRIMARY SOURCE HISTORY OF THE PILGRIMS' JOURNEY TO THE NEW WORLD

J. POOLOS

rosen central
Primary Source™

The Rosen Publishing Group, Inc., New York

Published in 2004 by The Rosen Publishing Group, Inc.
29 East 21st Street, New York, NY 10010

Library of Congress Cataloging-in-Publication Data

Poolos, J.
The Mayflower: A primary source history of the Pilgrims' journey to the New World / by J. Poolos. — 1st ed.
    p. cm. — (Primary sources in American history)
Summary: Uses primary source documents, narrative, and illustrations to recount the history of the Pilgrims' journey to America in search of religious freedom, their struggle to survive, and their encounters with native people as they worked together to build a successful colony.
Includes bibliographical references and index.
ISBN 0-8239-4514-6
1. Pilgrims (New Plymouth Colony)—Juvenile literature. 2. Mayflower (Ship)—Juvenile literature. 3. Massachusetts—History—New Plymouth, 1620-1691—Juvenile literature. 4. Pilgrims (New Plymouth Colony)—History—Sources—Juvenile literature. 5. Massachusetts—History—New Plymouth, 1620-1691—Sources—Juvenile literature. [1. Pilgrims (New Plymouth Colony)—History—Sources. 2. Mayflower (Ship) 3. Massachusetts—History—New Plymouth, 1620-1691—Sources.] I. Title. II. Series.
F68.P75 2003
974.4'8202—dc21

2003009877

Manufactured in the United States of America

On the front cover: *The Mayflower on Her Arrival in Plymouth Harbor*, an 1882 painting by William Formsby Halsall. Courtesy of the Pilgrim Hall Museum.

On the back cover: First row (left to right): committee drafting the Declaration of Independence for action by the Continental Congress; Edward Braddock and troops ambushed by Indians at Fort Duquesne. Second row (left to right): the *Mayflower* in Plymouth Harbor; the Oregon Trail at Barlow Cutoff. Third row (left to right): slaves waiting at a slave market; the USS *Chesapeake* under fire from the HMS *Shannon*.

CONTENTS

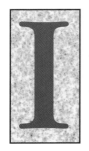

INTRODUCTION

When we think of the *Mayflower*, we think of the first Thanksgiving and of the coming together of the Pilgrims and the Indians. We think of turkey, cornucopias of vegetables, and polished black shoes with buckles. But the story of the *Mayflower* goes far beyond these symbols. It's about a small group of people who were abused by a government that did not respect their beliefs. It's about devotion in the face of religious intolerance, courage during a deadly voyage over the ocean, and determination against sickness and starvation.

THE SPIRIT OF INDEPENDENCE

The Pilgrims endured these hardships so that they could have religious freedom. They most likely had no idea how historically significant their struggles would become. In 1802, nearly 200 years after the *Mayflower* landed, Massachusetts senator John Quincy Adams saluted the Pilgrims in a speech entitled "Commemoration of the Landing of the Pilgrims": "[F]or the sake of reconciling their sense of religious duty with their affections for their country, few, perhaps none of them formed a conception of what would be within two centuries the result of their undertaking." The Pilgrims, he continued, were not "aware that they were laying the foundations of a power, and that [they were] sowing the seeds of a spirit." The spirit of which Adams spoke is the spirit of independence, which was to fuel generations of Americans to seek freedom no matter what the cost.

Brave enough to go where none had gone before, the Pilgrims gave up everything they had to start lives they hoped would be better. They were not seeking wealth or power. They simply wanted to live according to their own principles instead of those of their king and country. The remarkable character of this group of 100 or so individuals helped change the course of history.

TIMELINE

1492 — Christopher Columbus lands in the New World, discovering it for Spain.

1517 — Martin Luther nails his theological declaration to the castle door at Wittenberg, Germany, launching the Protestant Reformation.

1534 — Henry VIII issues the Act of Supremacy, declaring the king to be the supreme head of the Church of England.

1602 — John Robinson, Richard Clyfton, and their congregation flee England to Holland.

1606 — King James I grants a charter to the Virginia Company, a group of London entrepreneurs, to establish a settlement in North America.

August 5, 1620 — The *Mayflower* and the *Speedwell* set sail for Virginia.

November 1620 — Swept off course, the *Mayflower* anchors off Cape Cod.

TIMELINE

November 22, 1620 — Forty-one men, including William Bradford, John Alden, and Myles Standish, sign the Mayflower Compact.

March 22, 1621 — Pilgrims sign a peace treaty with the Wampanoag Indians.

May 1621 — John Peirce and the Merchant Adventurers Company create the Peirce Patent, securing the colonists' right to self-governance at Plymouth.

CHAPTER 1

SOWING THE SEEDS OF SEPARATISM

By the dawn of the seventeenth century, England had witnessed more than 150 years of religious unrest. Officially, England was a Catholic kingdom. But another Christian movement, already well established in other European countries, was beginning to catch on. Its advocates were called Protestants.

The Protestant movement in England took root in the Reformation, which came about in 1532 when King Henry VIII could not gain permission from the pope to annul his marriage to Catherine of Aragon. Because the Catholic Church forbade Henry to break the laws, the king separated England from Vatican rule, thereby opening the door for the Protestant movement.

Over the course of the century, England's official religious views continued to change, often swinging back and forth between the principles of Catholicism and those of the newer

King Henry VIII made a lasting mark on England and on Western Christianity. Obsessed with producing a male heir, he adjusted English laws to suit his needs and separated the country from the Catholic Church. Although he is best known for having six marriages, Henry VIII was loved by his people and was considered a great leader. This oil-on-wood portrait was painted around 1536 by German artist Hans Holbein the Younger, who was famous for his paintings of the Court of Henry VIII.

Protestantism. Queen Mary I reversed King Henry's ruling and allied England with the Catholic Church, only to see her successor, Queen Elizabeth I, break from it again. But in 1604, King James I reestablished England's ties with the Vatican with unbridled conviction. To show his allegiance to the church, he openly persecuted Protestants. Protestant leaders were forced to preach to their congregations in secret or risk a punishment such as a jail sentence.

The Forming of Separatism

Protestants in England had divided into two religious groups by the early seventeenth century. Although they had differences in their outlook as to how the Church of England should be changed, both groups sought the same basic goals. The majority group was called the Puritans, based on their desire to purify the church of nonessential elements. In other words, the Puritans were more or less happy with the idea of a state church, so long as both the state and the church conducted all business according to the scriptures, rather than according to current politics or personal agendas. They considered many of the behaviors and practices associated with Catholicism, such as honoring the king or queen as one would honor a deity, as sacrilegious notions.

The second group was called the Separatists. This group was formed by Protestant religious leaders who accepted that the Church of England would never adopt the Puritan beliefs. These leaders and their congregations separated from both the church and the Puritan extremist group, believing that purification was impossible and that the church was beyond repair, no matter how hard the Puritans worked for reform. Ministers John Robinson and Richard Clyfton and their congregations practiced Separatism.

Painted by artist Charles Lucy, *Departure of the Pilgrims from Delft Haven* shows the Separatists in Holland before embarking on their journey to the New World. The painting was created around 1847 and is part of the Pilgrim Hall Museum in Plymouth, Massachusetts. Minister John Robinson is shown at the painting's center, arms outstretched, leading the band of Leiden Pilgrims in prayer.

The Separatists had no faith that a national church could change to their satisfaction. They worshiped in the English town of Scrooby, at the private residence of Separatist William Brewster. Because the king did not allow separation from the church, they were persecuted and sometimes arrested. With nowhere to turn the Separatists fled to Amsterdam, Holland, in 1607, where they joined several other groups of English emigrants. But after about a year, religious disagreements drove them to move inland to Leiden, Holland, where they adopted their name, the Leiden Pilgrims.

The Pilgrims found stimulation at the university in Leiden and the intellectual communities that surrounded it. But they were forced to take low-paying jobs to support themselves. This, coupled with the impending threat of an attack on Holland by Spain, motivated them to move to another part of the world. They had heard of the settlements in the wilderness across the Atlantic Ocean in the New World, those settled by John Smith and the Virginia colonists in Jamestown in 1602. Despite the hardships they had heard about in Jamestown, they began to consider what life would be like in a society of their own creation.

In his journal, prominent Pilgrim William Bradford described the Separatists' plight and their consensus on the risks of traveling to largely uncharted lands:

> Though they should loose their lives in this action, yet might they have comforte in the same, and their endeavors would be honourable. They lived hear but as men in exile, & in a poore condition; and as great miseries might possibly befale them in this place, for ye 12. years of truce [the truce between Holland and Spain] were now out, & ther was nothing but beating of drumes, and preparing for warr, the events wherof are allway uncertaine.

So with a greater freedom in mind, Robinson, Clyfton, Brewster, and the rest of the congregation began making plans to secure financing for the epic voyage to Virginia.

CHAPTER 2

Once the Leiden Pilgrims decided to leave Holland for the New World, they approached investors for funding. After being turned down in Holland, they found investors in London who represented the Merchant Adventurers Company. It was agreed that the investors would fund the voyage, and the Pilgrims would repay the debt with raw materials from Virginia. What this meant to the Pilgrims was that everything in their new colony would be partly owned by the investors for seven years. This included all personal property, land, buildings, livestock, and profits earned through trading or selling. After seven years, the property would be divided among the investors and the Pilgrim shareholders. This arrangement put the Pilgrims into significant debt, yet they gained a necessary asset: funding for their trip. With this cash advance, the Pilgrims could purchase passage and enough food and provisions for their first year in America.

PLANNING THE VOYAGE

With the agreement reached, two ships were hired—the *Speedwell* and the *Mayflower*. Little is known about the *Speedwell*, other than its cargo capacity was approximately 60 tons, one-third the capacity of the *Mayflower*.

The *Mayflower*

The *Mayflower* was not built as a passenger vessel but as a cargo ship. Its accommodations were tailored toward crew and cargo. Instead of cabins and a dining room, it had a hold (an area of a ship belowdecks) for the Pilgrims' supplies and a room above the hold approximately 60 feet (18 meters) long by 30 feet (9 m) wide, where the Pilgrims all lived together. Conditions were cramped, and privacy was not an option. Nonetheless, the cargo ship was less expensive to hire for the voyage, and the Pilgrims were willing to forgo comfort for their dream of religious freedom.

The first known record of the *Mayflower* is from the summer of 1609. The ship was used to transport goods from England to France and Spain. Its primary ports of call were Bordeaux and La Rochelle, France. It commonly carried textiles, fox and rabbit furs, and iron and pewter utensils, and returned with French wine.

No exact drawings or diagrams of the *Mayflower* exist, and the exact dimensions of the ship are not known. Some sources estimate the distance from the back rail to the end of the bowsprit was 113 feet (34 m), and the length of the keel was 64 feet (20 m). The cargo capacity is estimated at 180 tons.

Passengers and Crew

The *Mayflower*'s passenger list was made up of residents of England. Most of the passengers in this London group had ties to the investors who were funding the new settlement in Virginia. Some were relatives of the members of the Leiden Pilgrims, some believed in the Separatist ideal, and others just wanted to start a new life.

The *Mayflower*'s crew consisted of between twenty and thirty members. Notable crew members include Christopher Jones, who owned a quarter share of the ship and was the ship's master. He

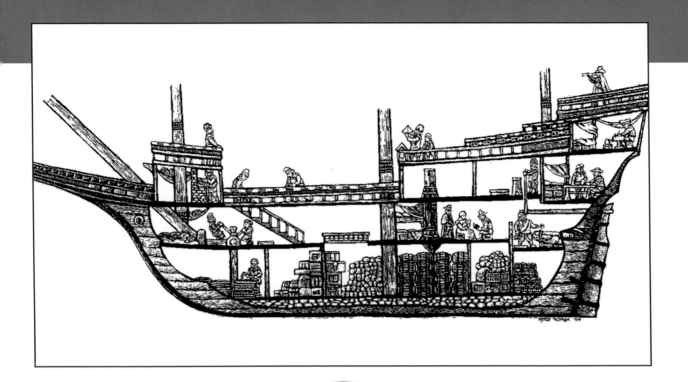

This diagram was created for the *Mayflower II*, the full-scale reproduction of the original *Mayflower* ship that carried the Pilgrims to Massachusetts. The passengers made their cabins in the "'tween decks" *(center right)*, which they shared with livestock, guns, and parts of the shallop. A British group built the *Mayflower II* from historically accurate materials in 1955 and two years later sailed it to Plymouth, Massachusetts, where it is open to visitors.

functioned as the captain, as he had when the *Mayflower* transported cargo to and from France and Spain. His mates were Robert Coppin and John Clark, who was a frequent voyager to Virginia. In 1611, Clark had been captured by the Spanish, imprisoned in Havana, Cuba, and then in Seville and Madrid, Spain. When he was released, he served as ship's pilot on a different vessel, traveling to Jamestown, Virginia, before being hired on the *Mayflower*. The ship's surgeon was Giles Heale. John Alden was the ship's cooper, responsible for the building and maintenance of the ship's barrels, where liquids and dry goods were stored. Alden was one of the rare crew members who stayed on at the new settlement when the *Mayflower* returned to England.

Myles Standish, a professional soldier, was hired as a military consultant and advisor. As a lieutenant in Queen Elizabeth's army, Standish was stationed in Holland, where he befriended John Robinson and got to know the Pilgrims in Leiden. He would prove to be one of their most important figures.

How We Know About the Pilgrims

It was the custom of the Pilgrims to document their arrangements. All official agreements were put into writing. In addition to these documents, several sermons, journals, and collections of personal letters remain. These writings document various periods and subjects associated with the *Mayflower* voyage and the establishment of their settlement, Plymouth Colony. In addition, some of the original Pilgrims left wills. Some of the most informative examples of Pilgrim writings are the following.

- *A Relation or Journal of the Beginning and Proceeding of the English Plantation Settled at Plymouth,* various authors. Sometimes known as *Mourt's Relation*, referring to the name G. Mourt, the signature beneath the book's dedication. G. Mourt was probably George Morton, who came to Plymouth Colony on the *Anne* in 1623. This series of journals includes firsthand accounts of the Pilgrims' early adventures.

- *Of Plymouth Plantation,* William Bradford. A firsthand account of the Pilgrims, beginning with the voyage on the *Mayflower* and ending with the first Thanksgiving.

- *New England's Salamander Discovered,* Edward Winslow. A famous essay and sometimes scathing attack on the colony's critics.

- **The Mayflower Compact.** A temporary agreement to govern as a body.

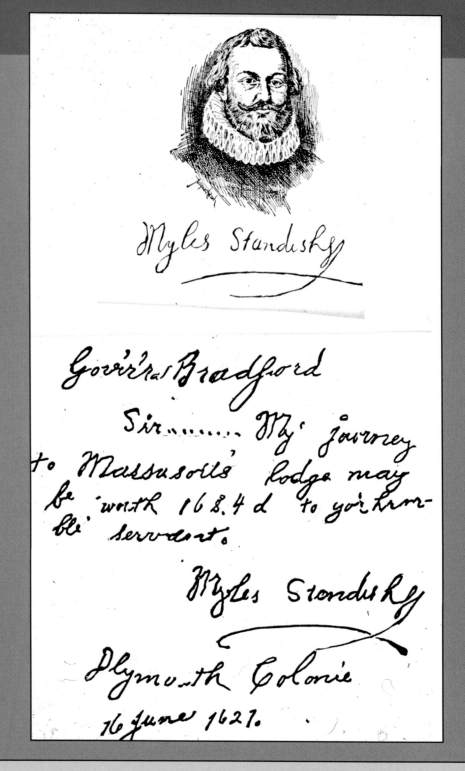

Myles Standish wrote this note to Governor William Bradford on his personal stationery on June 16, 1621. Standish served in England's army and assumed a position of leadership within the Pilgrim community. His military expertise was called upon when the colony required defense against the Indians.

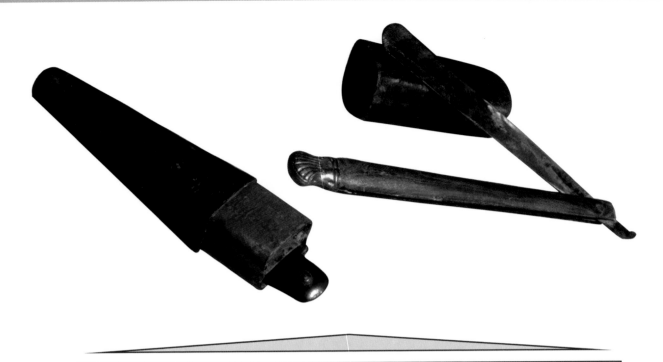

This shaving razor and case are believed to have belonged to Myles Standish. They were found at the site of the Standish House in Duxbury, Massachusetts, and are now in the permanent collection at the Pilgrim Hall Museum. The steel, horn, and brass razor is dated 1612 on the blade and was most likely manufactured in Toledo, Spain. The case is made of pasteboard that was painted and stamped to look like leather. Experts believe that Standish carried this razor on the *Mayflower*.

- **Peace Treaty with Massasoit.** The result of the meeting in 1621 between the chief of the Pokanoket Indians and the Pilgrim leaders.
- **The Peirce Patent.** The document in which England authorizes the Pilgrims to settle a self-governed colony in Plymouth.

Packing for the New World

The Pilgrims had to pack provisions both for the voyage to the New World and for their first year as settlers. They would need to build homes and other structures, plant and harvest

This chair was made in Plymouth Colony around 1630 and was part of a pair owned by Governor William Bradford. It was constructed from black ash wood. The artifact was passed down through generations of the Bradford family to the Hedge family, who donated it to the Pilgrim Hall Museum, where it now resides. From restoration over the years, the chair has lost three inches in height and is missing its hand grips. In addition, the seat, top crest rail, and several spindles have been replaced.

crops, and hunt wild game. The provisions they brought from England included food staples, household implements, tools, and firearms. With two ships and approximately 100 passengers, the Pilgrims would have enough supplies to begin their settlement.

A list of provisions was drawn up by Edward Winslow. All individuals and families were encouraged to provide the food, spices, clothing, arms, tools, and household implements Winslow had named. Also included on the list as "other things necessary to be taken over to this Plantation" were books, nets, hooks and lines, cheese, bacon, and goats. The Pilgrims hoped that once the colony was established other ships would bring cattle, pigs, and hens.

Stocked with equipment and provisions, the Pilgrims would set out for the New World, where they could practice their religious beliefs, free of persecution from English authority. William

Among the items the Pilgrims were encouraged to bring with them to the New World were cooking pots and tools. The cast-iron pot in this photograph belonged to Myles Standish and was passed down through his family. It is now on display in the Pilgrim Hall Museum. Made in England around 1600, the pot was probably used to make pottage, an English stew.

Bradford, the eventual governor of the new colony, summarized the opposing feelings of gravity and hope in his journals:

All great & honourable actions are accompanied with great difficulties, and must be both enterprised and overcome with answerable courages. It was granted ye dangers were great, but not desperate; the difficulties were many, but not invincible.

CHAPTER 3

In July 1620, the *Mayflower* sailed to Southampton, a busy port to the south of London. There it met the *Speedwell*, which had carried the Separatists from Holland. Once the final arrangements were made, John Robinson boarded the ship and read an inspirational letter he had written encouraging the voyagers to look to God in the face of the inevitable hardship.

The journey got off to a rocky start. After two emergency dockings due to serious leakage on the *Speedwell*, it was agreed that the ship was not in sufficient shape to make the voyage safely. Other than the approximately twenty passengers who decided to remain in England, all the *Speedwell*'s passengers boarded the *Mayflower*, their provisions packed into the hold. On September 6, 1620, for the last time, with a count of 102 passengers, the *Mayflower* set sail for the New World.

DEPARTING ENGLAND

Speedwell passenger Robert Cushman wrote of the troubles in a letter to his friend, Edward Southworth, on August 17, 1620.

Our pinnace will not cease leaking, else I think we had been half-way to Virginia. Our voyage hither hath been as full of crosses as ourselves have been of crookedness. We put in here to trim her; and I think, as others also, if we had stayed at sea but three or four hours more, she would

The Pilgrims set out from Southampton, England, in the chartered *Mayflower* and the smaller *Speedwell*, which they owned. It wasn't long before they had to abandon and sell the leaky *Speedwell* and squeeze extra passengers on board the *Mayflower*. This oil painting shows the two ships anchored in Dartmouth Harbor, where the *Speedwell* was repaired. Marine artist Leslie Wilcox painted the scene in England in 1971.

have sunk right down. And though she was twice trimmed at Hampton, yet now she is as open and leaky as a sieve; and there was a board a man might have pulled off with his fingers, two foot long, where the water came in as at a mole hole. We lay at Hampton seven days in fair weather, waiting for her, and now we lie here waiting for her in as fair a wind as can blow, and so have done these four days, and are like to lie four more, and by that time the wind will happily turn as it did at Hampton. Our victuals will be half eaten up, I think, before we go from the coast of England, and if our voyage last long, we shall not have a month's victuals when we come in the country.

Cramped Quarters

For the first week, the *Mayflower* enjoyed strong winds and made steady progress without event. The passengers had found the cargo vessel's living quarters cramped, but with the addition of the *Speedwell*'s passengers, living conditions were a true test of patience. Passengers set up living quarters in the ship's 'tween deck, the room typically used to hold cargo. There were no walls or dividers to provide privacy. Men, women, and children of all ages—many strangers at this point in the voyage—lived elbow to elbow, knee to knee. The occasional rat would emerge from the ship's hold, looking for a scrap, for each passenger or family had its provisions for the voyage close at hand.

The close living caused some discomfort and some more serious problems. It was one thing to read, eat, and sleep in a small room with a low ceiling among 100 other people, none of whom had bathed in some time—the air was hot and stale, and carried a sour odor. But when the seas grew rough and the *Mayflower* was tossed about on the waves of storms, things took on quite a different light. Seasickness was a regular event for nearly every passenger. It wasn't long before the sour odor became a horrendous stench and the air was barely breathable.

Only one primary source account of the voyage exists. In his book *Of Plymouth Plantation*, William Bradford documents the journey's conditions and events. About the first death on the *Mayflower*, he wrote:

And I may not omit here a special work of God's providence. There was a proud and very profane young man, one of the sea-men, of a lusty, able body, which made him the more haughty; he would always be condemning the poor people

The names of those which came over first, in ye year 1620. and were by the blesing of god) the first beginers, and (in a sort) the foundation, of all the plantations, and Colonies, in New-Englande (and their families)

mr John Caruer.
kathrine his wife:
Desire minter: &
2. man-seruants
John Howland
Roger Wilder·
William Latham, a boy.
& a maid seruant: & a
child y was put to him
called. Jasper More

mr William Brewster.
Mary his wife, with
2. sons, whose names
were Loue, & Wrasling.
and a boy was put to
him caled Richard More, and another
the rest of his children
were left behind & came
over afterwards.

mr Edward Winslow
Elizabeth his wife, &
2. men seruants, caled
georg Sowle, and
Elias Story; also a litle
girle was put to him caled
Ellen, the sister of Richard
More·

William Bradford, and
Dorathy his wife, hauing
but one child, a sone left
behind, who came afterward·

mr Isaack Allerton, and
Mary his wife; with 3. children
Bartholmew
Remember &
Mary· and a seruant boy.
John Hooke·

mr Samuel fuller; and
a seruant, caled
William Butten· His wife
was behind, & a child, which
came afterwards·

John crakston and his sone
John crakston

Captin myles Standish
and Rose his wife.

mr Christopher martin,
and his wife; and 2. seruants,
Salamon prower, and
John Langemore

mr William mullines, and his
wife; and 2. children
Joseph, & priscila; and a seruant
Robart Carter.

mr William White, and
Susana his wife; and one sone
caled Resolued, and one Borne
a ship-bord caled perigreene; &
2. seruants, named
William Holbeck, & Edward Thomson

mr Steuen Hopkins, &
Elizabeth his wife. and 2.
children, caled giles, and
Constanta a doughter, both
by a former wife. and 2. more
by this wife, caled Damaris, &
Oceanus, the last was borne at
sea. and 2. seruants, called
Edward Doty, and Edward Litster.

mr Richard Warren, but his
wife and children were left
behind and came afterwards

John Billinton, and Elen his wife;
and 2. sones John, & francis.

Edward Tillie, and Ann his wife;
and 2. children that were their
Cosens; Henery Samson, and Humil.
ity Coper

John Tillie, and his wife; and
Elizabeth their doughter

This is the passenger list from the *Mayflower* journey to the New World. The list was divided into party groupings. Each family was logged in as one entry, such as in the case of notable Pilgrim Edward Winslow, who was entered along with his wife Elizabeth and their children; two manservants, George and Elias; and a little girl named Ellen. The list appears in William Bradford's account of the Pilgrim settlement, *Of Plymouth Plantation*.

in their sickness, and cursing them daily with grievous execrations, and did not let to tell them that he hoped to help to cast half of them overboard before they came to their journey's end, and then to make merry with what they had; and if he were by any gently reproved, he would curse and swear most bitterly. But it pleased God before they came half seas over to smite this young man with a grievous disease, of which he died in a desperate manner, and so himself was the first that was thrown overboard. Thus his curses light on his own head; and it was an astonishment to all his fellows, for they noted it to be the just hand of God upon him.

Heavy Seas

Though the *Mayflower* made good progress, it wasn't long before harsh crosswinds and storms lashed the vessel. Already a well-used ship, the *Mayflower* began to leak. Eventually, a main beam in the middle of the ship cracked, and the crew feared the ship would not make it to Virginia. The crew was able to support the broken beam with a large iron screw and a post. They then caulked the area around the beam to waterproof it. The violent winds and high seas continued for weeks. At one point the crew took down the sails so the ship wouldn't be torn apart. In effect, this tactic took control of the ship out of the crew's hands and left it to the mercy of the wind and sea.

During one storm, the seas were so rough that a young man named John Howland was swept overboard by a large swell. He was somehow able to grab hold of the topsail halyards that hung over the side of the ship and into the water. As he clung to the ropes, the *Mayflower* pulled him deeper and deeper underwater, until finally the ship rose on another swell, and he was pulled back up to the surface, where other crew members used a boat hook to help him aboard.

With all the storms, Captain Jones and his mates assumed the *Mayflower* had been blown far off course. How far, they did not know. When eventually the seas calmed and the skies grew clear, they were able to determine their approximate position. And not long after, on November 9 (according to some accounts), they spotted land.

Finally, it was the New World—not Virginia, but Cape Cod, in present-day Massachusetts. At once they attempted to sail south to the mouth of the Hudson River, near what is now Long Island, New York. But after nearly being shipwrecked on dangerous shoals called Tucker's Terror, they decided to return to Cape Cod to explore the area. Once they had completed their evaluation, they could decide to stay or to continue their voyage to Virginia.

CHAPTER 4

It had taken the *Mayflower* sixty-six days to cross the Atlantic—more than two months of hunger and hardship. Cape Cod was cold, and snow covered the sand dunes on the beach. Captain Jones sent out a search party led by military consultant Myles Standish to survey the area to see if it was suitable for a colony. However, they could not find a good water source, and the soil looked too poor to grow crops. They returned to the *Mayflower*, but not before raiding a supply of corn that the Indians had stored underground near several grave markers.

LANDING AT PLYMOUTH

Over the next few weeks, similar parties would survey the cape and the near shore. But they soon began to run low on both supplies and morale. One of the *Mayflower*'s crew, the pilot, Robert Coppin, had visited the area on another voyage. He was familiar with a nearby bay he thought would show more promise as an area for a settlement. The natives called the bay Patuxet. Captain John Smith, a well-known explorer, had renamed it Plymouth Bay when he mapped the area several years before.

Making the Mayflower Compact

Once the *Mayflower* sailed into Plymouth Bay, the Pilgrims decided that attempting to sail to their Virginia destination

Painted by Haverhill, Massachusetts, native Henry A. Bacon, *The Landing of the Pilgrims* depicts the arrival of the *Mayflower* passengers in the New World. At the painting's center, fifteen-year-old Mary Chilton steps onto Plymouth Rock. The gray sky and the snowy, rocky shore show that the Pilgrims did not arrive to a welcoming landscape and hints at the continued hardships to come. The painting is oil on canvas and was created in 1877.

would be too risky. They decided to settle in the first suitable area they found. However, this decision presented a problem: They had been granted a settlement in northern Virginia, but this authorization to settle did not apply to Cape Cod or to anywhere else, for that matter. In effect, the Pilgrims had no legal right to establish an official governing body that would make important decisions. At the same time, there had been some general disagreement among certain passengers during the voyage. Several of the passengers looked at the lack of an official government as an opportunity for independence from the group, while others urged the rest to work together toward common goals. In *Of Plymouth Plantation*, William Bradford wrote:

facte by them done (this their condition considered) might
be as firme as any patent; and in some respects more sure
The forme was as followeth.

In ye name of god Amen. we whose names are underwriten
the loyall subjects of our dread soueraigne Lord king James
by ye grace of god, of great Britaine, franc, & Ireland king.
defendor of ye faith, &c

Haueing undertaken, for ye glorie of god, and aduancemente
of ye christian faith, and honour of our king & countrie, a voyage to
plant ye first Colonie in ye Northerne parts of Virginia. Doe
by these presents solemnly & mutualy in ye presence of god, and
one of another, Couenant, & Combine our selues togeather into a
Ciuill body politick; for our better ordering, & preseruation & fur=
therance of ye ends aforesaid; and by vertue hearof to Enacte,
constitute, and frame shuch just & equall Lawes, ordinances,
Acts, constitutions, & offices, from time to time, as shall be thought
most meete & convenient for ye generall good of ye Colonie: unto
which we promise all due submission and obedience. In witnes
wherof we haue hereunder subscribed our names at Cap=
Codd ye 11. of Nouember, in ye year of ye raigne of our soueraigne
Lord king James of England, franc, & Ireland ye eighteenth
and of Scotland ye fiftie fourth. An: Dom. 1620.]

After this they chose, or rather confirmed Mr John Carver (a man
godly & well approued amongst them) their Gouernour for that
year. And after they had prouided a place for their goods, or
comone Store, (which were long in unlading for want of boats,
foulnes of ye winter weather, and sicknes of diuerce) and begune
some small cottages for their habitation; as time would admite
they mette and consulted of lawes, & orders, both for their
ciuill & military Gouernmente, as ye necessitie of their condition did require, still adding therunto as urgent occasion
in seuerall times, and as cases did require.

In these hard & difficulte begininngs they found some discontents
& murmurings arose amongst some, and mutinous speeches & cariage
in other; but they were soone quelled, & ouercome, by ye wis:
dome, patience, and just & equall carrage of things, by ye Gou:
and better part weh claue faithfully togeather in ye maine.
But that which was most sadd, & lamentable, was, that in 2.
or .3. monethts time halfe of their company dyed, espetialy
in Jan: & february, being ye dept of winter, and wanting
houses & other comforts; being Infected with ye scuruie &

The original 1620 Mayflower Compact no longer exists. The image shown
above is from Governor William Bradford's account of the Pilgrims' story, *Of
Plymouth Plantation*. The Pilgrims drew up this document when their plans
changed and they landed in Massachusetts instead of Virginia. The document
is transcribed on page 58 of this book.

Philadelphia artist Edward Percy Moran (1862–1935) painted *The Signing of the Compact in the Cabin of the Mayflower* around 1900. It is now part of the collection of the Pilgrim Hall Museum. The scene shows Myles Standish *(center)* watching William Bradford *(right)* sign the Mayflower Compact. William Brewster and John Carver sit at the table beside them on board the *Mayflower*.

. . . occasionally partly by the discontented and mutinous speeches that some of the strangers amongst them had let fall from them in the ship; that when they came ashore they would use their own liberty, for none had power to command them, the patent they had being for Virginia and not for New England, which belonged to another government, with which the Virginia Company had nothing to do.

There was a great potential for disharmony, and the possibility of the group dividing into opposing sides was something the Pilgrims were forced to consider.

The leaders held a meeting in which they restated their mission, to pursue the ideals of liberty and equality for all men. They remembered their faith in God and all the reasons they had fled England and Holland. As a solution to their dilemma, they drafted a contract, a statement that spelled out in broad terms their plan to work together as a single group. The contract was the Mayflower Compact, perhaps the first example of government in America. Forty-one men, including William Bradford, John Alden, and Myles Standish, signed the Mayflower Compact on November 22, 1620. This was to be a temporary means of keeping all individuals working together to contribute to the new settlement.

Finding a Home

The crew continued to send search parties out to explore the lay of the land and to make contact with the Native Americans, with whom they hoped to trade for food and seed. In their explorations they found various markers in the ground. They made a habit of digging around these markers, often finding supplies the Native Americans had stored. Being devout Christians, the Pilgrims were not likely to steal. Yet because they had so little food and seed with which to plant crops in the spring, they confiscated the stores of corn, wheat, and beans, hoping to pay back the natives at a later date. Bradford wrote, "And sure it was God's good providence that we found this corn, for else we know not how we should have done, for we knew not how we should find or meet with any Indians, except it be to do us a mischief."

In late November 1620, the first Pilgrim birth in the New World occurred when William and Susanna White had a son

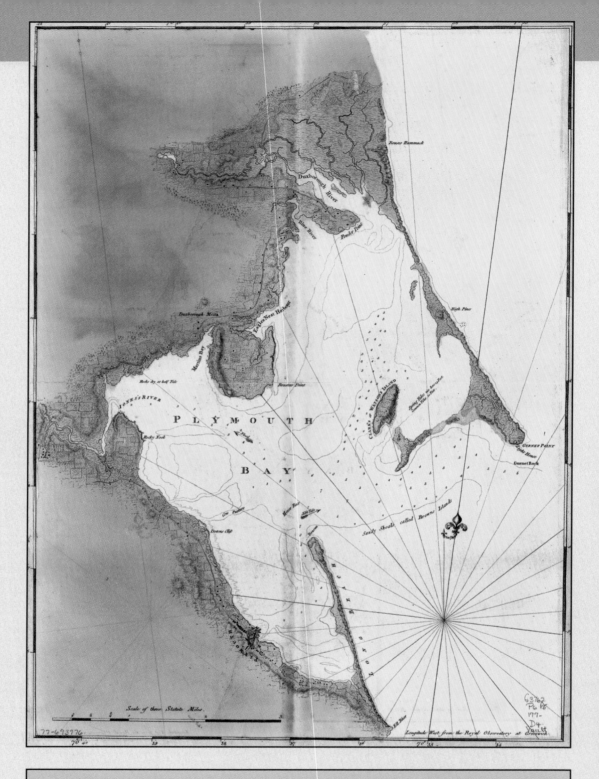

This seventeenth-century chart shows Plymouth Bay, off what is now Cape Cod, Massachusetts. In the midst of their stormy journey, the Pilgrims on the *Mayflower* were blown off course. Instead of reaching the established colony of Virginia, they arrived at a point farther north on the East Coast. Desperate, sick, tired, and hungry, they decided to stay at Cape Cod and build a settlement there.

they named Peregrine. (A baby was born on the journey over, to Elizabeth Hopkins. She named him Oceanus.) It was also at this time that a search party made first contact with the Indians. The Pilgrims had risen at dawn to prepare for exploration, when one of the men sighted a group of Indians emerge from the woods. Just then, the arrows began to fly around them. William Bradford recounted "the cry of our enemies was dreadful, especially when our men ran out to recover their arms; their note was after this manner, 'Woach woach ha ha hach woach.'" The Pilgrims took up their muskets and fired into the woods where the natives took cover. Eventually, the Indians retreated, and the Pilgrims fired their muskets into the air and shouted as one—in part to celebrate the defeat of their attackers and in part to show the Indians they were not afraid.

On December 9, a party set out in a shallop (a small boat) for Thievish Harbor, so named because in Robert Coppin's earlier days some rough sailors had stolen a harpoon from them near there. A storm raged and snapped the shallop's mast, but Coppin was able to set the boat on a sandbar near a tiny island. The party weathered the stormy night there, as well as the next day. Eventually, they sounded the harbor, looking for rocks, sandbars, and shallows, then went ashore to explore. There they found many cornfields, several running brooks, and a suitable area for building. They returned to the *Mayflower*, where they decided to settle in the area they had just surveyed.

At last the Pilgrims had found a new home. After several months on the *Mayflower*, all were lifted by the prospect of hard work and by putting the most difficult part of their journey behind them.

CHAPTER 5

Faith alone provided the strength to survive what was perhaps the most devastating winter in the history of North American colonization. The Pilgrims and crew lived out of the ship for a few months while the first buildings of the colony were constructed. Every day they made trips inland to work on their houses and storehouses. It was the beginning of the next phase of hardship for the Pilgrims. The misery that had been fueled by seasickness and cramped quarters was now fed by sub-zero temperatures, hard labor, hunger, and the fear of the Indians they would most certainly encounter. William Bradford summarized the challenges the Pilgrims faced in their struggles: "Constructing homes and storehouses proved to be very slow going: many were sick and could not labor hard; bad weather frequently prevented much work from being done; and the few structures they did build occasionally succumbed to fire."

MEETING THE NATIVES

Though weak and discouraged, they soldiered on, while more and more of them grew sick and died. In *The History of the United States*, Julian Hawthorne states, "That winter they put up with much labor a few log huts: but their chief industry was the digging of clams and graves." By the spring of 1621, of the 102

This 1876 engraving shows Samoset entering Plymouth Colony to meet the Pilgrims. Note the frightened expression on the Pilgrim woman's face. Samoset belonged to an Algonquin tribe in southern Maine, where he learned English from European fishermen. He was visiting Massasoit when he encountered the Pilgrims. Samoset proved to be a great help to the Pilgrims, introducing them to other Indians who would help them survive in the New World.

passengers that made the voyage on the *Mayflower*, only 52 had survived. Yet the work got done. Besides building shelter, the Pilgrims constructed a shed for their common provisions, and they prepared against attack from the Indians.

Meeting Samoset

On the morning of March 16, 1621, the Pilgrims made the breakthrough for which they had been waiting uneasily all these months. While going about their daily chores, the Pilgrims were caught off guard by an Indian who walked boldly up to the edge of the village. To their surprise, the Indian greeted them in English.

Pilgrim William Bradford's Geneva Bible is shown above. It is now part of the collection of the Pilgrim Hall Museum. Published in 1592, the Bible is an accurate representation of those kept in every Pilgrim household. Their faith and devotion to God were what brought the Pilgrims to the New World and also what got them through the difficulties of their journey and settlement. The Geneva Bible was considered the most accurate English version of the Bible at that time.

This man was named Samoset. He explained that he had learned to speak English from some men who came to fish at Monchiggon (present-day Monhegan Island, Maine). He appeared to be familiar with European customs. He told the Pilgrims that he had been sent by the great Massasoit, *sachem* (chief) of the Pokanoket, to welcome them and to arrange an alliance. He told of the great plague four years earlier that had wiped out the native population of the area, which he called Patuxet. Samoset stayed the night and in the morning left with gifts, promising to return with more Pokanoket in a few days.

Samoset kept his word, and after several visits, the Pilgrims and the Indians began to build a trust. Each party was fairly confident

Interview with Massasoit, painted by Eastman, shows Pokanoket leader Massasoit (1590–1661) and his men meeting with the Pilgrims. The Pokanoket were part of a larger tribe called the Wampanoag, or People of the Dawn. Archaeological findings indicate these people lived in the New England area for some 10,000 years. Their nation stretched from what is now Boston northward to Narragansett Bay, Rhode Island.

that the other had no hostile interests. Samoset introduced them to another Indian who spoke English. Tisquantum, sometimes called Squanto, was a native Patuxet who had lived in England for a number of years.

In 1614, when Tisquantum was a young man, he was one of a few dozen Indians engaged in trade with Captain John Smith, who had come to New England to map Cape Cod. When Smith departed, a captain named Thomas Hunt kidnapped twenty-four Indians and sailed them to Spain to be sold as slaves. In Malaga, Spain, friars took some of the Indians, sparing them from slavery. From there Tisquantum sailed to England, where he began to learn the English language. He was given a job as interpreter at a colony on Newfoundland called Cupper's Cove. While there he met a captain named Thomas Dermer. Dermer worked for the New England Company, which had interests in establishing a profitable fur trade in the New World. He thought Tisquantum could be invaluable in establishing relations and commerce with the Indians, so he sailed Tisquantum back to England and then on to Patuxet, where Tisquantum's journey had begun. They arrived to find all of Tisquantum's tribe dead of a plague.

Tisquantum searched out Massasoit, who took him in. The Pilgrims arrived that year, and Tisquantum was instrumental in their initial treatise with the Indians. He also taught the Pilgrims how to best use their natural resources. He continued to help William Bradford and other Pilgrim leaders negotiate with the Indians until he died in 1622.

The Peace Treaty with Massasoit

On March 22, Massasoit and his sixty men appeared on a hill near the village. He wanted to engage the Pilgrims in a peace accord. Myles Standish led the Pilgrim delegation. The two parties approached each other cautiously, eventually exchanging hostages as a sign of good will. The leaders went into a building in the village, and after sharing food and drink, they began to discuss a mutually beneficial relationship. After some time, they wrote out an agreement that satisfied the interests of both parties:

1. That neither he nor any of his should injure or do hurt to any of our people.
2. And if any of his did hurt to any of ours, he should send the offender, that we might punish him.

This painting, *Treaty with the Indians*, by artist Botkin, shows Pilgrim leaders meeting with Massasoit and his men. The two groups came together to sign a peace treaty that would prove to be beneficial for everyone. The agreement bound the Pilgrims and the Wampanoag to live together peacefully. This helped the Pilgrims to successfully settle in the New World. The alliance also helped the Indians stand up to stronger tribes in the region.

3. That if any of our tools were taken away when our people are at work, he should cause them to be restored, and if ours did any harm to any of his, we would do the likewise to them.

4. If any did unjustly war against him, we would aid him; if any did war against us, he should aid us.

5. He should send to his neighbor confederates, to certify them of this, that they might not wrong us, but might be likewise comprised in the conditions of peace.

6. That when their men came to us, they should leave their bows and arrows behind them, as we should do our pieces when we came to them. Lastly, that doing thus, King James would esteem of him as his friend and ally.

This photograph shows a scene of Plimoth Plantation, in Plymouth, Massachusetts. Plimoth Plantation, which functions as a living history museum, is a reconstruction of the original Pilgrim village. The village includes a main street bordered by accurate reproductions of Pilgrim houses and gardens. Community structures are located throughout, including an outdoor oven, meeting house, cow house, and hay house. Staff members dress in period clothing and take on the identities of the original Pilgrims to give visitors an accurate idea of what Plymouth Colony was like. Rounding out the experience are nearby reconstructions of a Wampanoag homesite and the *Mayflower*.

This agreement would mean safety and trading for the Pilgrims. But for Massasoit it would mean much more. By showing that he was not afraid of the white man, he gained the respect and loyalty of his tribe. At the same time, an alliance with gun-bearing Englishmen would make the tribe less vulnerable to the powerful Narragansett Indians to the south. It was a strategic move made by a savvy leader, and it would benefit the Pokanoket in more than one way.

CHAPTER 6

TWO HARVESTS

With the new treaty and the onset of warmer weather, the Pilgrims' spirits were lifted. It had been a brutal winter with much sickness. Of the 102 passengers that made the voyage on the *Mayflower*, only 52 survived. Most of the dead had succumbed to typhoid, scurvy, or pneumonia. Now that winter was over and the Pilgrims had settled in their new home, the *Mayflower* could return to England. Unfortunately, the Pilgrims had no fish, furs, or lumber to send back with the ship. Thus, the merchants with whom the Pilgrims had arranged the voyage would see no profit this year. Nonetheless, on April 5, 1621, the *Mayflower* set sail. It carried letters telling of the success of the colony at Plymouth and of the abundance of resources.

The *Mayflower* arrived in England on May 6, 1621. The journey was made in less than half the time it took to sail from England to Cape Cod the previous September. Once the news got out that the Pilgrims had started the colony at Plymouth and not in Virginia, the investors who had supported the voyage sprung into action to make the settlement legitimate in the eyes of the English government.

The original patent specified a settlement in Virginia. Now that the Pilgrims were in Plymouth, the Virginia patent was

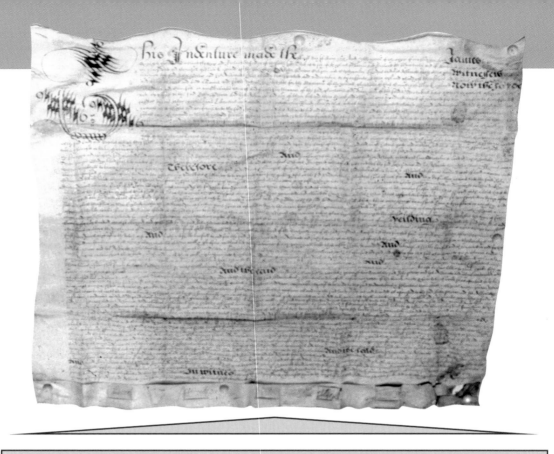

When the Leiden Pilgrims found financial backers in the Merchant Adventurers Company in England, the investors of the Virginia Company issued Merchant Adventurers a patent to start a new settlement in Virginia. This patent was the (First) Peirce Patent, also known as the Virginia Patent. When the *Mayflower* was blown off course and the Pilgrims decided to settle in Massachusetts, the patent didn't apply, since that area was out of the bounds of the Virginia Company. The Second Peirce Patent, shown above, was later issued in acceptance of the Pilgrims' settlement in Plymouth. A transcription of the document appears on page 58 of this book.

invalid. And although the Pilgrims created the Mayflower Compact in order to grant themselves the right to govern themselves, they required official authorization. So the Merchant Adventurers, the investors who held stock in the Plymouth Colony, sent a representative named John Peirce and a small delegation to the Council of New England to secure official recognition of the settlement. Specifically, they asked that the Pilgrims be granted the right to establish a

It is believed that Pilgrim William White and his pregnant wife, Susanna, brought along this cradle on the *Mayflower* journey. Their son was born on the *Mayflower* as it sat in Provincetown Harbor in November 1620. They named the child Peregrine, which means "Pilgrim" or "traveler." The cradle is now part of the collection at the Pilgrim Hall Museum. It is important because it shows that the Pilgrims came to the New World with a commitment to making lives for themselves and raising their families there.

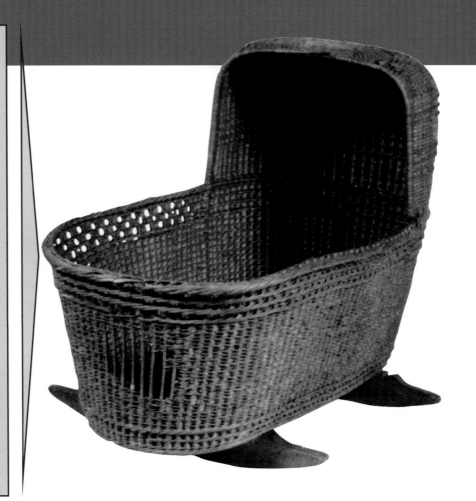

government based on their own beliefs and values. As a result, the Peirce Patent of 1621 was drafted. It replaced the Virginia patent, and it replaced the Mayflower Compact as the ruling document at Plymouth.

Now Plymouth was a legal English settlement, free to trade and conduct commerce and entitled to all rights and privileges of English citizens. In simple terms, England had granted the Pilgrims permission to stay in Plymouth. In terms of their place in history, the Pilgrims had achieved religious independence from the Church of England and were living their lives according to their principles, not those of the English throne.

This same month John Carver, who was governor of the colony, became gravely ill and died. William Bradford recounted the incident in *Of Plymouth Plantation*:

Governor William Bradford owned this silver cup and brought it with him on the *Mayflower* journey to the New World. The cup was handmade in London in 1634 and is now co-owned by the Pilgrim Hall Museum and the National Museum of American History in Washington, D.C. Seven inches (17.8 centimeters) in height, the cup bears the engraved initials "W. B." on one side.

In this month of April, whilst they were busy about their seed, their Governor (Mr. John Carver) came out of the field very sick, it being a hot day. He complained greatly of his head and lay down, and within a few hours his senses failed, so as he never spake more till he died, which was within a few days after . . . And his wife, being a weak woman, died within five or six weeks after him.

Shortly after Carver's death, William Bradford himself was chosen as the next governor. Because he had been sick a good deal of the winter, he was weak, and Isaac Allerton was appointed his assistant.

The First Thanksgiving

As the snow melted away, the Pilgrims sowed seed, and they continued to prepare more fields for crops. Through the spring and summer they toiled, planting crops, hunting, and gathering food. The game was abundant, and the fish were plentiful. Tisquantum was an invaluable source of information. He showed the Pilgrims how to plant corn on hills, using fish as fertilizer. He also showed

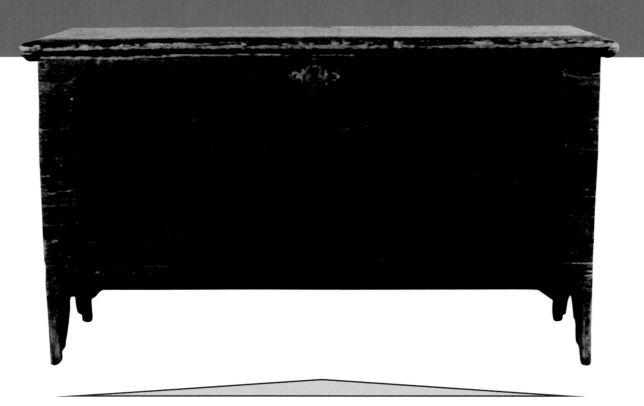

Another artifact that made the *Mayflower* journey with the Pilgrims was William Brewster's wooden chest, shown above. Measuring 30 inches (76 cm) high, 50.5 inches (130.8 cm) wide, and 19 inches (48.3 cm) deep, the chest was made from Norway pine and iron in the early seventeenth century. It is believed the chest was made in Holland, carried to England on the *Speedwell*, and brought to the New World on the *Mayflower*. Although relatively large in size, chests were important and versatile possessions to bring to the New World. They could be used as storage, tabletops, sleeping spaces, and seating.

them the best places to hunt and fish. Thus, the Pilgrims shot deer, waterfowl such as ducks and geese, and wild turkey. They also caught large numbers of cod and bass, among other fish.

By summer's end, the Pilgrims harvested their crops and began to prepare for winter. The wheat and barley crops were not very bountiful, but the corn crops were very successful. They were so successful that it was estimated there would be enough corn to feed both the Pilgrims and the Indians through the coming winter. This kind of success in a fledgling settlement

This painting imagines the first Thanksgiving between the Indians and the Pilgrims. Painted by Jennie A. Brownscombe (1850–1936) in 1914, long after Plymouth Colony, *The First Thanksgiving at Plymouth* shows a peaceful gathering between the two parties. Brownscombe used some details that are not historically correct, such as the log cabin shown on the right and the feathered headdress worn by the Indians. But the portrayal of devotion, community, and celebration struck a chord with many Americans, and the painting was published in the popular American magazine *Life*.

was unheard of. It can be attributed in part to the decision made by Governor Carver and leaders at Plymouth regarding the parceling of land. Colonies such as Jamestown in Virginia had common plots. That is, all men worked together at community plots. At Plymouth, Carver gave each man or family a plot of his own on which to work. This plan proved to be a much more efficient means of food production.

As was the tradition in Europe, the Pilgrims held a harvest celebration in the fall of 1621. This was the first Thanksgiving Day. All the colonists participated, as did Chief Massasoit and

This portrait of Pilgrim Edward Winslow (1595–1655) is the only likeness of a Pilgrim painted from life. The oil portrait was created by an unknown artist in London in 1651. After settling in Plymouth, Winslow made many trips back to England. He brought the first cattle to America. An important member of the colony, Winslow served as governor and also as an ambassador to the Wampanoag. He eventually returned to live in England, leaving his wife, Susanna White Winslow (mother of Peregrine White, the first child born to the Pilgrims in the New World) behind. In the painting, Winslow holds a letter signed "From yr loving wife Susanna."

ninety Wampanoag men whom Governor Bradford invited as a gesture of goodwill and coming together. Much game and fish were consumed over the three-day feast, which served to lift the morale of the colonists. The Indians presented five deer to Bradford, Captain Jones, and others. Edward Winslow wrote in *Mourt's Relation*:

> Our harvest being gotten in, our governor sent four men on fowling, that so we might after a special manner rejoice together, after we had gathered the fruits of our labors . . . and although it be not always so plentiful, as it was at this time with us, yet by the goodness of God, we

A RELATION OR

Iournall of the beginning and proceedings of the English Plantation setled at *Plimoth* in NEW ENGLAND, by certaine English Aduenturers both Merchants and others.

With their difficult passage, their safe ariuall, their ioyfull building of, and comfortable planting themselues in the now well defended Towne of NEW PLIMOTH.

AS ALSO A RELATION OF FOVRE

seuerall discoueries since made by some of the same English Planters there resident.

I. In a iourney to PVCKANOKICK *the habitation of the Indians greatest King* Massasoyt : *as also their message, the answer and entertainment they had of him.*

II. *In a voyage made by ten of them to the Kingdome of* Nawset, *to seeke a boy that had lost himselfe in the woods : with such accidents as befell them in that voyage.*

III. *In their iourney to the Kingdome of* Namaschet, *in defence of their greatest King* Massasoyt, *against the* Narrohiggonsets, *and to reuenge the supposed death of their Interpreter* Tisquantum.

IIII. *Their voyage to the* Massachusets, *and their entertainment there.*

With an answer to all such obiections as are any way made against the lawfulnesse of English plantations in those parts.

LONDON,
Printed for *Iohn Bellamie*, and are to be sold at his shop at the two Greyhounds in Cornhill neere the Royall Exchange. 1622.

Mourt's Relation was published in 1622 in England. The pamphlet was composed of firsthand accounts of the Pilgrims' first year in Plymouth Colony. The accounts were overwhelmingly positive, with stories of the difficult journey, illness, starvation, danger, and death conveniently left out. The idea was to paint the Pilgrims' year in the New World as a success and to encourage more people to join them.

are so far from want, that we often wish you partakers of our plenty.

As the feast marked the fruitful harvest, it also marked the end of the growing season. With this, the Pilgrims began to prepare for winter, boarding up their windows with shutters and preparing food stores for the impending cold season. They had survived the most difficult phases of their relocation, securing England's authorization to settle in Plymouth, building a town, establishing relationships with the Indians, and growing their first crops. These were confidence-inspiring accomplishments that reminded the Pilgrims just how far they had come from their days on the *Mayflower*.

CHAPTER 7

THE PILGRIMS BEYOND THANKSGIVING

Not long after the first Thanksgiving feast, the Pilgrims took inventory of their harvest and found they had overestimated their supplies. They were forced to cut their weekly food rations in half. Then on November 20, 1621, the Pilgrims had surprise visitors. The *Fortune*, a ship sailing from England, arrived at Plymouth with thirty-five new colonists who wished to live there. Unfortunately, the original Pilgrims were unprepared for the new arrivals. Having built only seven houses, they lacked sufficient living quarters. To make matters worse, the *Fortune*'s passengers came without food and supplies, and they appeared to lack the discipline shared by the Leiden Pilgrims. William Bradford wrote:

They were lusty young men, and many of them wild enough, who little considered whither or about what they went. But there was not so much as biscuit or cake or any other victuals for them, neither had they bedding, but some sorry things they had in their cabins; not a pot nor pan to dress any meat in; nor over many clothes. The

This bronze statue of William Bradford was created by artist Cyrus Dallin in 1921. It was commissioned for the Plymouth Colony's 300th anniversary and stands on Water Street in Plymouth, Massachusetts. Bradford served many years as governor of Plymouth Colony. Orphaned as a boy, Bradford became a Separatist when he was twelve. On the *Mayflower* journey, his wife fell overboard and drowned, but he later married a woman who traveled to the New World on the *Anne*. After all he had seen the Pilgrims endure, Bradford was sad to see the colony break up when many Pilgrims decided to venture off in search of more land.

Plantation was glad enough of this strength, but could have wished that many of them had been of better condition, and all of them better furnished with provisions.

Nonetheless, they made accommodations, all looking with some dread to a winter of hunger and deathly sickness. The next month, the *Fortune* was on its way back to England, carrying the text of *Mourt's Relation*, perhaps one of the two most significant firsthand accounts of early Pilgrim life. The ship left its passengers, and as the colonists were forced to supply the *Fortune* with food from their stores, they were left with even less to survive the winter.

The Hardship Continues

Though the colonists had been promised ships sending food from England, they never came. By May they had completely emptied their food stores. The fowl were in short supply in the warm months, and the colonists lacked the proper equipment to fish for cod. However, they were able to catch shellfish with their hands and stay alive by their nourishment. As the next harvest was four months away, Edward Winslow made a 150-mile (241.4-kilometer) trip up the Maine coast to try to obtain provisions. There were English ships in the area, and the colonists had hopes he would not return empty-handed. Several ships provided him with bread and other provisions free of charge, which the colonists rationed among themselves.

During the spring and summer months, the Pilgrims had little time in the fields. They were occupied building a fort for defense against possible attack in case the Indians should turn on them. All summer they lacked sufficient food, and they were often too weak to work the long hours necessary for a successful harvest. As a consequence, the harvest of 1622 did not meet their needs. As things were looking especially desperate for the upcoming winter, the English ship *Discovery* sailed into Plymouth with a cargo of knives and beads that they could use in trade with the Indians for food.

But the trinkets didn't last, and for the third straight year the Pilgrims faced a winter without sufficient food. They lived on a diet of deer, fowl, and occasionally fish. They also ate nuts and berries. Yet they lacked vegetables, as well as milk, butter, and oil. The shallop was converted into a fishing boat, and the Pilgrims sent shifts of men out so the boat was fishing at all times of the day. Thus, they were able to keep themselves supplied with fish, eating the occasional deer or turkey when possible.

Again, spring brought the planting season, and again the Pilgrims were weak from a lack of food. June brought a drought that lasted six weeks, and the crops began to wilt. Desperate, the Pilgrims gathered one morning in July and prayed for nine hours. The next day it rained, and the rain came for two straight weeks. The crops were revived, and the Pilgrims were more hopeful than ever.

At about the same time, two ships, the *Anne* and the *Little James*, arrived from England with a full stock of provisions and sixty settlers to further populate the colony. With the help of new healthy workers and their supplies, the harvest of 1623 was a huge success. It marked the turning point for the original colonists, who had struggled from the first days on the *Mayflower*, and who had now proven they could reap a bountiful harvest from the land.

The Pilgrims had borrowed a good deal of money and had assumed a heavy debt. With the increased population, they began to procure more and more raw materials that would have value in England. Their chief crop was corn, and they traded it with the Indians for beaver and otter furs, which in England were quite valuable commodities. They also shipped back timber and fish, which were also in demand. However, some of the ships carrying the raw materials were lost at sea or captured by pirates. Ships that did deliver the goods often carried representatives from Plymouth. These men returned to the colony with shoes, tools, and domestic goods. Eventually they brought over cattle and other livestock.

Beginning to Thrive

By the mid-1620s, the Pilgrims had turned the colony at Plymouth into a viable business operation. Because they were earning such profits, they decided to pay off their seven-year debt to their investors. The Peirce Patent had allotted 100 acres (40.5 hectares) of land to each settler for whom the Merchant Adventurers Company paid passage. Any profit borne of the land was to be shared by the company and the colony, and at the end of the seven-year period all assets would be divided among the shareholders, including the Pilgrims. In 1626, the Pilgrims negotiated an arrangement wherein fifty-three of the colonists would buy out the company over a two-year period. The sum they paid was 1,800 English pounds.

The Pilgrims also began to expand their trading business, engaging European colonies in exchanges of fur, corn, and fish for cloth and tobacco. Trade with the Indians continued to be productive for the Pilgrims. In his essay "A Letter Sent from New England," Edward Winslow wrote, "We have found the Indians very faithful in their Covenant of Peace with us." This relationship

This hat was made in England in the early 1600s from beaver fur. England imported fur from the colonies, which were rich with many resources unavailable in Europe. Pelts were processed into felt used to make hats and other articles of clothing. The colonies remained a source of valuable goods for England until they gained independence in 1776.

was to last more than fifty years. The Indians had plenty of furs to trade for corn and for tools made in England. The colonists were also interested in buying more land, and the Indians were willing to sell. Thus the physical dimensions of the colony grew by leaps and bounds. More new colonists would arrive in the next few years. By 1626, Plymouth's population would grow dramatically.

Those numbers would grow even more dramatically over the next fifteen years, as ships full of colonists were making the voyage from England. In 1628, Puritans sailed to Massachusetts and settled in Naumkeag, which is Salem, Massachusetts, today. Two years later, John Winthrop arrived in Massachusetts. He was the bearer of the Massachusetts Bay Charter, a certificate authorizing him to establish a colony in the New World. Many Puritans joined Winthrop in founding Boston.

By the late seventeenth century, English colonists had taken over the New England seaboard, having firmly entrenched themselves both physically and in matters of trade. The area was what in another generation would become the United States of America.

It is difficult for most of us to comprehend the achievements of the Pilgrims. To imagine being persecuted for our beliefs to

These 1651 oil portraits from the Pilgrim Hall Museum represent the next generation of Pilgrims. Shown on the right, Josiah Winslow (1628–1680) was born to Pilgrims Edward and Susanna Winslow. He served as Plymouth governor from 1673 to 1680. While visiting England, he married aristocrat Penelope Pelham (1630–1703), who had lived in America for a brief time as a young girl. She is shown on the left. The portraits show the couple to be wealthy, elegant, cultured, and fashionable. One can see how different life was for Plymouth families after just one generation. More important, these portraits represent the fruits of all the labor and hardships endured by the first Pilgrims.

the point that we would give up our homes—in some cases, our families—to move to a faraway, unsettled territory is to imagine a modern-day United States intolerant of our beliefs and desires. Our America is not like the England from which the Pilgrims came. Unlike John Robinson and the other Separatists, we are free to worship as we wish, to meet with whomever we want. We have the Pilgrims to thank for that. Their struggles on the *Mayflower* and in Plymouth Colony proved that faith, the promise of religious liberty, and perseverance against all odds are enough to seed a nation.

PRIMARY SOURCE TRANSCRIPTIONS

Page 29: Excerpt from the Mayflower Compact

Transcription

In the name of God, Amen. We whose names are underwritten, the loyal subjects of our dread sovereign lord King James, by the grace of God, of Great Britain, France, and Ireland King, Defender of the Faith, etc.

Having undertaken, for the glory of God, and advancement of the Christian faith, and honor of our king and country, a voyage to plant the first colony in the northern parts of Virginia, do by these presents solemnly and mutually in the presence of God and one of another, covenant, and combine ourselves together into a civil body politic, for our better ordering and preservation, and furtherance of the ends aforesaid; and by virtue hereof to enact, constitute, and frame such just and equal laws, ordinances, acts, constitutions, offices from time to time, as shall be thought most meet and convenient for the general good of the colony: unto which we promise all due submission and obedience. In witness whereof we have hereunder subscribed our names; Cape Cod, the 11th of November, in the year of the reign of our sovereign lord King James, of England, France and Ireland eighteenth and of Scotland fifty-fourth, Anno Domini 1620.

Page 42: Excerpt from the 1621 Second Peirce Patent

Transcription

This Indenture made the First Day of June 1621 And in the yeeres of the raigne of our soueraigne Lord James by the grace of god King of England Scotland Fraunce and Ireland defendor of the faith etc. That is to say of England Fraunce and Ireland the Nynetenth and of Scotland the fowre and fiftith. Betwene the President and Counsell of New England of the one partie And John Peirce Citizen and Clothworker of London and his Associates of the other partie Witnesseth that whereas the said John Peirce and his Associates have already transported and vndertaken to transporte at their cost and chardges themselves and dyvers persons into New England and there to erect and built a Towne and settle dyvers Inhabitantes for the advancem[en]t of the generall plantacon of that Country of New England Now the sayde President and Counsell in consideracon thereof and for the furtherance of the said plantacon and incoragem[en]t of the said Vndertakers haue agreed to graunt assigne allott and appoynt to the said John Peirce and his associates and euery of them his and their heires and assignes one hundred acres of grownd for euery person so to be transported . . .

In witnes whereof the said President and Counsell ha[v]e to the one part of this p[rese]nte Indenture sett their seales And to th'other part hereof the said John Peirce in the name of himself and his said Associates ha[v]e sett to his seale geven the day and yeeres first aboue written.

[signed] LENOX HAMILTON WARWICK SHEFFIELD FERD: GORGES

GLOSSARY

alliance An association between two or more parties.

annul To declare invalid.

bowsprit A large mast projecting from the front of a ship.

cornucopia A horn overflowing with fruit and flowers to show prosperity.

covenant A usually formal, solemn, and binding agreement.

deity A god.

extremist One who advocates radical political or religious measures.

keel The long part of a boat along the bottom that extends from one end to the other.

patent An official document conferring a right or privilege.

persecution Suffering because of one's beliefs or causing someone to suffer because of his or her beliefs.

principles Rules and standards by which people live.

providence Divine guidance or care.

Reformation A movement in sixteenth-century Europe that established Protestantism.

sachem The chief of a confederation of the Algonquin tribes of the North Atlantic coast.

shallop A dinghy with one or more masts.

Vatican The papal headquarters in Rome.

victuals Food.

 OR MORE INFORMATION

Web Sites
Due to the changing nature of Internet links, the Rosen Publishing Group, Inc., has developed an online list of Web sites related to the subject of this book. This site is updated regularly. Please use this link to access the list:

http://www.rosenlinks.com/psah/mayf

 OR FURTHER READING

Deetz, James, and Patricia Scott Deetz. *The Times of Their Lives: Life, Love, and Death in Plymouth Colony*. New York: W. H. Freeman, 2000.

Demos, John. *A Little Commonwealth: Family Life in Plymouth Colony*, 2nd ed. New York: Oxford University Press, 1999.

Morison, S. E. *The Story of the Old Colony of New Plymouth, 1620-1692*. New York: Knopf, 1956.

Usher, Roland. G. *Pilgrims and Their History*. New York: Macmillan, 1918.

Willison, G. F. *Saints and Strangers*. New York: Ballantine Books, 1965.

BIBLIOGRAPHY

Adams, John Quincy. "Oration at Plymouth." Reprinted in the *Daily Republican*, December 22, 2002 (http://www.dailyrepublican.com).

Bradford, William. *Of Plymouth Plantation*. New York: McGraw-Hill, 1981.

Hawthorne, Julian. *The History of the United States from 1492 to 1920*. New York: P. F. Collier, 1920.

Logan, Samuel T. "The Pilgrims and Puritans." *Tabletalk Magazine*, Vol. 20, No. 11, November 1996.

"Mayflower, Pilgrims, Plymouth." encyclopedia.com. Retrieved February 13, 2003 (http://www.encyclopedia.com).

Stratton, Eugene Aubrey. *Plymouth Colony: Its History and People*. Salt Lake City: Ancestry Publishing, 1997.

Winslow, Edward. *Good Newes from New England*. Bedford, MA: Applewood Books, 1996.

PRIMARY SOURCE IMAGE LIST

Page 9: Oil on oak portrait of Henry VIII. Painted by Hans Holbein the Younger circa 1536. Housed in the Thyssen-Bornemisza Collection in Madrid, Spain.

Page 15: Diagram of the *Mayflower II*, the 1950s reconstruction of the *Mayflower*. From the Plimoth Plantation in Plymouth, Massachusetts.

Page 17: Note to Governor William Bradford. Written by Myles Standish on June 16, 1621, on his personal stationary.

Page 18: Razor and case found at the site of the Standish House in Duxbury, Massachusetts. Housed at the Pilgrim Hall Museum in Plymouth, Massachusetts. Made of steel, horn, brass, and pasteboard in 1612, probably in Toledo, Spain.

Page 19: Governor William Bradford's chair. Made of black ash wood in Plymouth Colony around 1630. Housed in the Pilgrim Hall Museum in Plymouth, Massachusetts.

Page 20: Cast-iron cooking pot. Descended from the Myles Standish family. Made in England around 1600. Housed at the Pilgrim Hall Museum in Plymouth, Massachusetts.

Page 24: The *Mayflower* passenger list from 1620.

Page 29: The Mayflower Compact, written in 1620. Published in *Of Plymouth Plantation*, by William Bradford.

Page 32: Chart of Plymouth Bay. Created by Joseph Frederick Wallet Des Barres in London in the eighteenth century. From the Library of Congress Geography and Map Division.

Page 36: William Bradford's Geneva Bible. Published in 1592. From the Pilgrim Hall Museum in Plymouth, Massachusetts.

Page 42: The 1621 Peirce Patent. Issued by the Merchant Adventurers Company in England. From the collection at the Pilgrim Hall Museum in Plymouth, Massachusetts.

Page 43: Cradle brought over by the White family on the *Mayflower*. Made in Holland around 1620 of wicker, with oak rockers and maple strut. From the Pilgrim Hall Museum in Plymouth, Massachusetts.

Page 44: Silver cup owned by Governor William Bradford. Made in London, England, in 1634. Jointly owned and exhibited by Pilgrim Hall Museum in Plymouth, Massachusetts, and the Smithsonian Institution's National Museum of American History in Washington, D.C.

Page 45: Wooden chest owned by Wiliam Brewster. Probably made in Holland in the early seventeenth century. Constructed from Norway pine and iron. Part of the collection of the Pilgrim Hall Museum in Plymouth, Massachusetts.

Page 47: Portrait of Edward Winslow. Oil on canvas, painted by an anonymous artist in the school of Robert Walker. Painted in London in 1651. From the collection of the Pilgrim Hall Museum in Plymouth, Massachussets.

Page 48: *Mourt's Relation*, printed in London, England, in 1622. From the New York Public Library.

Page 55: Beaver hat. Made in England from around 1615 to 1640. Ownership attributed to Constance Hopkins. From the Pilgrim Hall Museum collection in Plymouth, Massachusetts.

Page 56: Portraits of Penelope Pelham Winslow and Josiah Winslow. Both painted in oil in London in 1651. From the Pilgrim Hall Museum in Plymouth, Massachusetts.

INDEX

About the Author
J. Poolos is a freelance writer who lives in Iowa City, Iowa. He has written many books for Rosen Publishing, including a biography of Jackie Chan and an account of the 1995 Sarin attack on the Tokyo subway.

Photo Credits
Cover and pp. 11, 18, 19, 20, 22, 28, 30, 36, 37, 39, 42, 43, 44, 45, 46, 47, 51, 55, 56 © Pilgrim Hall Museum; title page © Burstein Collection/Corbis; p. 9 © Francis G. Mayer/Corbis; pp. 15, 40 © Plimoth Plantation; p. 17 © Hulton/Archive/Getty Images; pp. 24, 29 courtesy of the State Library of Massachusetts; p. 32 Library of Congress, Geography and Map Division, p. 35 © Bettmann/Corbis; p. 48 courtesy of the Rare Books and Manuscripts Collection, New York Public Library Astor, Lenox, and Tilden Foundations.

Designer: Nelson Sá; Editor: Christine Poolos; Photo Researcher: Adriana Skura